SCHIRMER'S LIBRARY
OF MUSICAL CLASSICS

SERGEI RACHMANINOFF

Preludes
For the Piano

Op. 23 — 10 Preludes

Library Volume 1630

⟶ Op. 32 — 13 Preludes

Library Volume 1631

ISBN 0-634-01892-2

G. SCHIRMER, Inc.

DISTRIBUTED BY

7777 W. BLUEMOUND RD. P.O. BOX 13819 MILWAUKEE, WI 53213

CONTENTS

I

S. Rachmaninoff, Op. 32, Nº 1.

Allegro vivace.

II

S. Rachmaninoff. Op. 32, № 2.

Allegro scherzando

III

Allegro vivace.

S. Rachmaninoff. Op. 32, No 3.

IV

S. Rachmaninoff, Op. 32. Nº 4.

Allegro con brio.

V

S. Rachmaninoff, Op. 32. No 5.

VI

S. Rachmaninoff, Op. 32. № 6.

Allegro appassionato.

VII

S. Rachmaninoff, Op.32.№ 7.

VIII

S. Rachmaninoff, Op. 32. Nº 8.

IX

S. Rachmaninoff, Op. 32. No 9

X

S. Rachmaninoff, Op. 32. № 10.

L'istesso tempo.

XI

S. Rachmaninoff, Op.32.Nº11.

Allegretto.

XII

S. Rachmaninoff, Op. 32 Nº 12.

XIII

S. Rachmaninoff, Op.32 №13.